He Said,

She Said,

I Said

7 Keys to Relationship Success

Barbara J. Peters, RN, LPC

Published in the United States by BQB Publishing
(Boutique of Quality Books Publishing)
www.bqbpublishing.com

Printed in the United States of America

978-0-9831699-8-7 (p)

Library of Congress Control Number: 2011927405

Book design by Darlene Swanson • www.van-garde.com
Phil Winter, Photographer
Illustrations by Steve McGinnis

I lovingly dedicate this book to my grandchildren, Briana, Lexa, Katherine, and Dylan.

I wish one day each of you will find a beautiful, meaningful, and lasting relationship. I hope my book can be your guide as you journey on your path.

Also by Barbara J. Peters

The Gift of a Lifetime: Building a Marriage That Lasts

Contents

Acknowledgments

There are several people to thank for their expertise and commitment to the pages of *He Said, She Said, I Said*. They are acknowledged in no special order as each played a significant role in the evolution of this book, and without them, it would not have been possible for me to complete this work.

Alice Eachus, Editor/Writer

I want to thank Alice for her excellent editing and impeccable attention to detail. I appreciate her willingness to make manuscript changes at a moment's notice. I have the ability to think impulsively and sometimes expect immediate reactions, and I am in awe of Alice's understanding and acceptance of my unique personality quirks. She has been a pleasure to work with, and I appreciate her encouragement along this journey.

Terri Leidich, Publisher/Writer

I want to thank Terri for her enthusiasm, encouragement, marketing, and assistance in all areas of this book. I am grateful to her for trusting me and my knowledge of relationships. In many instances, Terri cheered me on as additional thoughts and concepts were brought to the table. She incorporated new ideas easily and effectively to bring new vision to my words.

Kelly Thrash, Author's Assistant and Good Friend

I want to thank Kelly for coming up with the wonderful title for this book. With her insightful naming, the entire format of the book changed. Along with her many talents, Kelly has been there to encourage and motivate me through the process it takes to write and publish a book.

My Clients

I also want to express my gratitude to the many couples that have shared their intimate stories with me and have shown me what's really important to make a relationship grow and flourish as the years pass.

Foreword

Relationships are complicated, people aren't perfect, and we can often each get caught in the narrow pathways of our own perceptions. When situations occur where opinions or points of view differ, a couple's connection can either be strengthened or weakened depending on how their differences are handled.

Two people come into a relationship with distinct ways of viewing and reacting to the world, and it is those views and reactions that often determine the way the couple relates to each other. While relationships have many facets, areas of challenge, or opportunities for growth, as a counselor specializing in couples' therapy, I most often hear questions and concerns about seven key areas: communication, trust, forgiveness, intimacy, acceptance, friendship, and love.

While these topics exist in every intimate relationship, they surface in different ways, and the perspectives and perceptions with which they are handled are as unique as each couple experiencing them. When problems occur, the answers and solutions can often be as simple as being willing to change one's perception and look at a situation in a new way, thus initiating a change in response. When a couple is caught in the dance of a relationship, it can sometimes be hard to recognize where they may be caught in the trap of what they *think* is occurring instead of stepping out of that mire to find out what is really going on.

The following pages are filled with real statements that people in relationships have made about different experiences and circumstances in their lives, all focusing on the seven key areas mentioned previously. Often, a couple's statements and the way they are individually viewing a situation are at the core of the problem. In my counseling practice, I offer a perspective or way of thinking that can open the door to new thoughts, behaviors, reactions, experiences; this same technique is used in the pages of this book.

Whether you are currently in a relationship, thinking about entering one, or are recovering from a breakup or divorce, the comments and information in this book can help you identify if some of your perceptions or thought patterns may be causing problems or hindering your ability to create your own healthy relationship and "happy ending."

Remember . . .

Watch your thoughts, for they become words.
Watch your words, for they become actions.
Watch your actions, for they become habits.
Watch your habits, for they become character.
Watch your character, for it becomes your destiny.

~ Unknown

Barbara J. Peters, RN, LPC

Relationship Maintenance Agreement

A maintenance agreement is a great way to show your commitment to building a strong, lasting relationship. Think of it as an insurance policy or spoken promise. While you may both think and feel the same sentiments, putting them into spoken and written words will help solidify your intentions, because, as the great quote that is included in the foreword of this books says, words become actions.

A maintenance agreement might sound like this:

> I agree to keep my relationship as my utmost priority and work on it every day. I will not allow any cause to be a reason to forget my agreement. It is my hope that my everlasting love for you, along with this agreement, will help us achieve a relationship that lasts a lifetime.

You can use these suggested words or use your own to convey a similar message. The purpose behind creating a relationship agreement is to put your thoughts and intentions into words you both can remember and use as your guide for everyday interactions.

Communication

Barbara Says:

It is not only the content of the message that matters;
it is the delivery that makes the difference.

He Said: I feel we have poor communication and our relationship is one-sided, focusing mostly on her needs.

I Said: Communication. We all want it, need it, and do it; but how we communicate and how effective it is for both partners varies. A large percentage of couples seeking counseling have issues around communication, and while it may not be "the real problem," it certainly is responsible for many areas of relationship conflict.

People sometimes have the misconception that talking is communicating, but many times that is far from the truth. Talking is often one-sided, whereas communication requires both speaking your thoughts and desires and then actively listening to what your partner is saying as well.

If your partner is doing all the talking, you very well may feel that your communication is one-sided. But step back a moment and see if you are contributing to the communication by offering your comments, thoughts, and experiences, and if you are truly listening to what your partner is saying. If trying to communicate with you is like talking to the wall because you don't indicate in any way that you are listening or are interested in what is being said, your partner might be doing all the communicating for both of you. Try participating. Comment on what your partner is saying and show interest in his or her experiences, thoughts, and concerns. You just might be surprised when he or she becomes more open to hearing what you have to say.

A good technique to use for encouraging open communication is to openly request information about what is being asked or told to you by your spouse or partner. You might say, "This is what I heard, is it correct?" This allows for additional clarification from your significant other. You can then offer, "Can you tell me more so I am sure I understand?" This will put you in a better place to respond appropriately.

When you are trying to communicate about an issue in your relationship, it is first necessary that both of you understand the issues needing attention. Stay away from blaming and withholding your feelings or ideas. When you take responsibility for actually stating what you need or identifying what concerns and bothers you, you increase the probability of getting your needs met and opening the doorway to productive interaction.

If you are guilty of doing all the talking with a mate who doesn't seem to want to communicate, try asking questions to find out what is going on with him or her instead of just talking about *your* feelings, thoughts, or needs. Remember, communication is a two-way street, and it takes both of you to create conversations that resolve issues, build rapport, and strengthen bonds.

She Said: I have plenty of needs, but I'm not sure how to ask for them, or if he even cares what they may be.

I Said: Are you afraid to ask to have your needs met by the one you love? Do you feel asking for more support, affection, sex, consideration, attention, or "me time" is selfish?

Do you have the common misconception that . . . "If he/she really loved me, my partner would know what I need or want without being told?"

Then again, perhaps you don't know exactly what you need, or perhaps you don't realize you are unhappy or anxious as the result of your unmet needs. You might be feeling tense or irritable because you haven't had a minute to call your own for weeks. But rather than recognize you are desperately in need of "me, myself, and I time," you get angry with your partner for forgetting to do a simple chore; thus the undone chore becomes the excuse or catalyst for creating upheaval in your relationship. It is better to own up to your personal need for a time of quiet self-renewal than take out your frustrations on your partner.

At other times, you may get so frustrated that you *demand* instead of ask for recognition and attention. The conversation might go something like this: "You spend too much time working on your old car (or trying new recipes) and not enough time paying attention to me!" By taking this approach, you are defeating your own purpose. Think about it, who would *want* to spend time with somebody who is nasty, blaming, and demanding? Would you?

Sometimes your needs could be sexual in nature and you might be embarrassed to admit you want more or varied sex; you may be afraid that asking for new techniques in the bedroom could be construed as criticism and cause even more problems. In cases like this, you could be clinging to the misconception that not talking about sex is better than saying anything. Yet if you want a healthy, connected sexual relationship with your partner, talking over your physical needs and wants is crucial.

The key to getting your needs and wants met is always honest, genuine, open communication. Yet it doesn't have to be a sit-down-at-the-kitchen-table conversation with a long list of wants and needs ready to be checked off. Instead, try being playful, even teasing, when talking about what you need to be happy and fulfilled—all done with a soft touch.

Remember, becoming comfortable asking for what you need and getting those needs met won't happen all at once; it will be a work in progress. A good way to start is with the want or need that is easiest for you to articulate. Why make it hard on yourself?

While you want to start off with the "easy stuff," make a list of the things that are the hardest to ask your partner to do for you. What are the topics that make you so uncomfortable that you would rather spend the rest of your life suffering with unmet needs before you could or would address them? These uncomfortable topics are the very things that are absolutely imperative to discuss. These unmet, undefined needs will always cause undue stress and impact your emotional state negatively. Instead of conceding to a failed relationship to avoid issues, try to view your life differently to make the modifications necessary to create change for the better.

Once you are able to communicate all levels of need to your partner—and be okay with taking care of yourself in the process—you will feel supported and cared for in your relationship.

He Said: I'm not really sure she loves me the way I love her, and because of that, I find myself holding back my feelings.

I Said: Have you ever felt you loved more than you were loved in return? If so, what did that feel like? Did you feel your expression of love was clear to your spouse or partner, but theirs wasn't clear to you? When you felt that way, did you make your feelings known to your spouse in a caring loving manner? If not, then why not?

Instead, did you just decide your spouse or partner wasn't putting forth equal effort to grow your relationship and then made the assumption that he or she didn't love you as much as you loved them? There is a fallacy in that thinking. No two people act or behave in the same way, and therefore they may have different ways of expressing love. Just because you are not recognizing those behaviors as statements of love doesn't mean they are not happening. Instead of assuming your partner doesn't love you as much as you love him or her, open up communication around the subject instead of closing down.

It is always good to communicate how you define love to your partner or spouse and then ask how they view a loving relationship. Asking questions is a sure way of finding out about the person you have chosen to make your life partner, as well as your lifelong friend.

The questions could be as simple as: "What are some of the things I do that let you know I love you?" "What are some of things you do to express your love to me?" You may be surprised by the answers, because behaviors you exhibit, which you probably consider extremely loving, might not be at the top of your partner's list. In turn, your partner's actions or words, which might not hold much significance for you, could be the very things they consider to be important gestures that show how much they love and care about you. It's all in the way we perceive things.

Because communication is sometimes easier between friends than it is with a partner, continue to work on being a friend to your partner as well as a lover. Communication on many levels will help you understand what your partner is thinking and feeling, as well as give you an opportunity to express your own needs.

She Said: It's really hard to feel loving toward him when he won't allow me to get close enough to see who he really is.

I Said: "So many believe that it is love that grows, but it is the *knowing* that grows and love simply expands to contain it. Love is just the skin of knowing." ~ *The Shack*, William Paul Young

It isn't just being with a person that expands love, it is getting to know who they are that allows love to grow. That's why it is so important that as a couple you take the time to talk and share your thoughts, feelings, fears, and vulnerabilities with each other. It is this sharing of who you really are at your core that will create an environment of knowing and intimacy.

When you don't share your thoughts and feelings with the one you've chosen to spend your life with, you are depriving him or her of the opportunity to really get to know you, to love you because of that experience, to celebrate the good times with you, and support you through the tough times. Without ongoing communication in your relationship, you will stay separate and unconnected. With open communication, you can get to know each other deeply, which opens the doors for love to expand.

For some people, sharing their private thoughts and feelings is not an easy process. Yet in every relationship, it is vitally important to create time for talking, sharing, and feeling safe enough to be vulnerable. Whether you have a date and linger over dinner to share your experiences of the week or schedule time each evening before you go to sleep for a meaningful conversation, it is important that "time to talk" becomes part of your routine.

If it is difficult for either of you to share your deep thoughts and feelings, start by telling your partner about one area of your life. Maybe you begin by talking about work, your children, your in-laws, or the goals and dreams you have for yourself or for the two of you as a couple. Start off by sharing thoughts and experiences that feel good for you, so the two of you can begin to bond and become used to sharing at these depths. Once you have established open communication and begin to know and love each other deeply, a feeling of safety will develop where you'll be able to talk about thoughts and feelings that are less than pleasant. Knowing someone well means knowing all of who they are—the happy thoughts and experiences along with the disgruntled or even angry ones.

Loving someone is all about getting to know him or her as he or she really is and it can create a bond that is strong enough to last a lifetime. A verse from a song that was popular in the 60s says it well, *"To know, know, know him, is to love, love, love him . . . and I do, and I do, and I do."*

He Said: I'm a man. We're not supposed to ask for help; we're supposed to be the strong one who helps others . . . especially the woman in our life.

I Said: How do you feel when you must ask, or choose to ask, your partner for help?

To help others, especially those we love, is a basic altruistic response—it makes us feel good. But, being put in a position where we need to ask for help sometimes makes us feel inadequate or uncomfortable, because we fear being considered lazy or needy. Often, talking about our need for help or support is one of the most difficult forms of communication we ever do, as our fear of being judged or refused is so strong.

Yet there is another side to asking for help that can aid in strengthening and deepening a relationship. Allowing the people in our lives the opportunity to offer their talents and gifts, as well as share their thoughts and experiences, can expand their own good feelings about themselves. Because helping someone else makes us feel good, giving the one you love the opportunity to help you is a way of allowing him or her to relish in their own strengths and talents, and see firsthand how they enhance your life.

As a man, if you never show need or vulnerability, you are

not letting your partner see all of who you are, which keeps her at arm's length on an emotional level. It can also create an environment where the woman in your life feels "less than" when she needs your help.

A healthy relationship is one in which both partners are willing to ask for help and know they will receive a loving, supportive response.

She Said: I want to talk with him about issues like the kids, his mother, and my frustrations about trying to have a career and be a good mom. But every time I try to bring up these subjects, he either closes down or gets angry. I don't want him to fix the problems; I just want to be able to talk with him about our lives.

I Said: There is always more to say about communication in a relationship. In fact, most of the couples I counsel report their communication is *way* off and they cannot discuss a wide number of topics any longer. Women often say they just want the men in their lives to listen, and the men seem to think that if their woman has a problem it's up to them to fix it. These mismatched desires often create high levels of frustration where the unspoken conclusion is that it's easier not to talk about the issues at all. Yet that is not the solution.

In his book, *How to Really Love the One You're With*, Larry James writes, "Know what you need from your relationship. Then proceed with confidence. Mutually discuss your needs." Sounds simple enough, but in order to follow this sage advice, it's imperative that you change your perception around what's happening between the two of you and to also look at the well-established differences between men and women. When women have an issue, they often just want someone to listen to their feelings about the matter. Often having their husband listen and offer some sympathetic comments is all it takes.

Yet for men, it seems to be in their DNA that when someone they love is upset about something, they immediately think it is up to them to make it better. In many cases, just acknowledging those differences can create open communication. For instance, a woman could begin a conversation with, "Honey, I'd like to talk to you about some concerns I have, but I'm not asking you to fix them, I just want to let you know what I'm feeling." Or if you genuinely want their help or opinion, the conversation could start with, "I've got some mixed feelings about the last visit from my mom and dad, and I want to know what you think."

From a man's standpoint, if you're not sure if the woman in your life just wants to talk or if she wants you to fix the problem, ask her a question like, "I hear your frustration about Ben not picking up his toys. Do you want me to step in and fix the situation? Or do you just need me to listen right now?"

As people are together over time and experience new challenges in their life, often their wants and needs wax and wane. A new job, new baby, a newly empty nest, or even aging or health problems will precipitate change, and the feelings, fears, and concerns that travel with them can create anxiety. In order to stay close and connected, it is necessary to share with each other how these swings are affecting you and your perception of the relationship. But those talks aren't going to happen unless you've developed a pattern of communicating that is respectful of each other. It is important that neither of you views communication exclusively as what *you* want to say. By definition, communication is an exchange between two people. It is not a lecture or soliloquy.

Trust and love between the two of you can be developed and strengthened no matter what challenges may occur when you are both willing and able to talk about anything and everything in your life, and know the other person is ready to hear you and respond to the best of their ability.

He Said: When she uses that tone of voice with me or puts her hand on her hip, I don't feel like her husband; I feel like her child, and I just close down.

I Said: With this couple, it became evident it wasn't just what the woman was saying that pushed her husband away from her, but rather how she said it—with both her words and body language. Her delivery did not create a positive environment for continued dialogues, and her tone of voice and stance did not encourage her spouse to respond in a good way. If she had a way of knowing how her body language made her husband feel, she would then have a chance to change her posture and delivery, which could positively impact their interactions.

It is possible to do just that. Taking the time and effort to learn your partner's needs and perceptions can go a long way in discovering how to productively and respectfully talk with each other. The keys for understanding what your partner might be thinking or feeling is to make sure you stay in the present, deal exclusively with the concern at hand, listen to words spoken, and watch physical responses. Don't let your mind think about what happened in the past or the last time you had a similar conversation. And don't make assumptions. Ask questions about how he or she is feeling, right then, in the moment, with that experience . . . and then really listen, watch, and care about what you are hearing and seeing. A person's facial expressions and body postures can often speak louder than words.

Additionally, make sure you pay close attention to your own body language and your tone of voice, as well as the words you use. Remember, communication is so much more than words, and if the way you deliver your words or present yourself isn't in alignment with what you are saying, your partner will hear the loudest statement. For instance, if you are saying loving words in a harsh tone of voice with body language indicating irritation, your significant other will "hear" the irritation much more than the actual words themselves.

The next time you and your partner are spending time talking with each other, take a moment to look at the way you stand. Then consider what your posture, hand movements, or arm position could be saying to him or her. Is your posture in alignment with the message you want to send? Or is it contradictory?

If you are the one who is feeling belittled by your partner's body language or tone of voice, your feelings should be addressed, preferably at a time when you are comfortably and genuinely sharing with each other. Sometimes body stance becomes a habit more than a reflection of what a person is feeling. Give your loved one an opportunity to make some changes in the way he or she speaks to you instead of just closing down.

In a relationship, each is responsible for how he or she responds, both as the one doing the talking and the one doing the listening.

She Said: I am majorly pissed off at him, yet I'm afraid to make emotional statements because of his outbursts, which cause our efforts at communication to escalate without resolution.

I Said: We all get angry, and we all argue with the people we love. While arguments can be beneficial because they allow us the opportunity to hear another point of view and challenge ourselves to grow and see things from a different perspective, anger not listened to and dealt with can be destructive.

When angry feelings aren't resolved but are left to fester and grow, resentment can develop into a simmering alienation that is never healthy. When you argue with your special someone, it is important to resolve the issue as quickly as possible; when that doesn't happen, resentment can grab hold rather quickly. Once a reality, resentment can be difficult to shake.

Because resentment can have long-term, negative effects, it is imperative that a couple never, ever hesitates to talk with each other about a concern that is bothering one of them. Acting quickly can save a situation from going sour fast, because pushing feelings down makes it impossible to work through conflict, and you or your partner can become trapped by negative thoughts and emotions.

When discussing anger-prone issues with each other, make sure you understand your partner's point of view and where he or she is coming from. Asking questions and really listening to the answers are always good ways to discover what someone is feeling and thinking. When your partner feels his or her thoughts and feelings are important to you, escalated anger can often be eliminated.

You might start with something like, "What is it you are angry at me about?" or "If I change my behavior about _____, will you let go of your anger?" Truly listening to answers and exhibiting concern for how your partner feels and then accepting his or her needs will quickly turn anger into an opportunity to draw closer.

It's also important that you each communicate your individual feelings and anger in a respectful manner and take responsibility for your own feelings. How or what you feel isn't your partner's fault, yet you have every right to "feel your feelings" as long as they are expressed in a manner that is not hurtful or harmful.

It is possible to express anger without yelling, screaming, or closing down; however, if heated discussions between you and your mate have a tendency to escalate, a good method of communicating these issues is to take turns telling each other how you feel. Make an agreement that each of you will get five or ten uninterrupted minutes to express yourself. The one talking must be willing to make "I" statements about what they are feeling, and the one listening needs to do just that—listen. When the first person is finished talking, the listener then reflects back what he or she heard, which gives the person who did the talking the ability to either affirm the listener heard correctly or to make another statement. Once that process is completed, it is the other partner's turn to talk and be listened to.

Anger is inevitable when people intimately share their lives, but how that anger is communicated can mean the difference between a long, healthy relationship and one that doesn't last.

He Said: I think I am communicating with her, yet it's not what she wants or needs, and I don't have a clue what to do differently.

I Said: Lack of or sparse communication is one of the most frequent problems couples bring to a therapist. The simple fact is that it is impossible to achieve intimacy without good, ongoing communication.

It is true that there are many different ways to send messages in a relationship. Some people are more direct and actually ask for what they need and offer their views and input without much coaxing. Others are less open and unable to find the words to express feelings. Upbringing and background can have a lot to do with how someone initially communicates with his or her spouse or partner, but over time, a good relationship requires that couples learn how to effectively interact and talk with each other. It can get really complicated when two people come from different areas of the country, have different value systems, or come from different cultures. Yet those differences must be bridged, or at least understood, in order for a couple to know each other well.

There are simple things to do to increase positive interaction between two people, and being receptive to hearing another's point of view tops the list. Changing your own perceptions can lead to ways of responding differently to situations you encounter. A whole new world, one you might like better, could open to you. But you'll never know if you don't listen and consider expanding your mind to new ways of thinking.

One of the techniques I often recommend for couples struggling with communication issues is something called mirroring or reflective listening where the listener tries to clarify, restate, or paraphrase what he or she hears the other person saying. This approach lets your significant other either confirm or deny that what you heard is what he or she was trying to say to you. It opens the door for both of you to get clear on what is really being discussed.

Along with using the mirroring approach, there are five essential components for effective communication:

1. Listening attentively to one another

2. Clearly stating the point, without filters

3. Choosing an appropriate response for the content

4. Delivering the response in a loving, but direct manner

5. Being open to renegotiation if necessary

The more you are able to communicate and really hear each other, the closer and more intimate you can become.

She Said: In general, we communicate well and get along just great, but then we hit a bad spot and our attempts at trying to talk about what's going on escalate to a huge fight.

I Said: Even if you and your partner communicate well most of the time, there will still be instances when it feels as though you don't know how to talk with each other, or that you don't even know each other very well at all. Don't panic; this is normal.

No two human beings can always understand each other or will always be able to communicate in healthy, productive ways. There will be times that attempts at talking will escalate into confrontations that don't seem to be going anywhere.

The important thing to do in circumstances like these is to recognize what's happening and call a "time out." Agree to disagree, and get space between you as couple. It could mean that you work in the garden while your partner curls up with a good book. Or maybe each of you could spend a little time apart with friends.

As long as you both understand the situation is not going to be resolved at that point in time and neither of you goes away angry or in a huff, there are times when "taking a time out" from communicating is the best solution.

When you are able to come together and communicate calmly, the problem can be discussed and resolved at that time. Taking a "time out" from discussing a heated topic is not the same thing as ignoring it, allowing it to fester, or allowing resentment to grow. Taking a "time out" means you have both acknowledged there is an issue that needs handling, yet recognized you are not in a spot to do it at the current moment.

He Said: In the beginning, it was really exciting when I discovered she liked chocolate ice cream, the Beach Boys, and primitive art, just like I did. Now we know everything about each other and the excitement is gone.

I Said: When we first begin to learn about the people who are destined to become our significant others or spouses, the gates are flung open and a rush of trivia—some good, some bad, and some downright ugly—floods our heads. We just can't learn enough about the person we find so attractive.

Somehow we tend to assume nothing changes as years pass, until one day we overhear our spouse telling an acquaintance, "My favorite ice cream is strawberry." What in blazes is going on here?

We sometimes forget that life and experiences change people, and what was once a reality for them no longer is. How well do you really know your spouse or significant other as he or she is today? Maybe it's time to find out and reignite the excitement of discovery you once experienced.

Turn off the television for an evening and try an experiment I often suggest to couples having a difficult time communicating with each other or those who have slipped into a routine of assuming they know all there is to know. All it takes is a pad of paper, pen, and a good dose of reality.

Each partner should jot down at least ten questions to ask the other, but both must answer to spread the wealth of knowledge sure to be discovered. Start with easy questions like "What's your favorite song, vacation, dessert?" and so on.

Then begin probing a little deeper . . . What are you passionate about? What do you fear the most? Who is your hero? Did you or do you have a mentor? All these questions will require thought and may take some time to answer. No rush; this should be a work in progress.

There is no score to tally; the goal is to learn more about who your partner is now, possibly discovering things and thoughts that might surprise you. It's fun to do, and you could uncover interests you never knew you shared.

Trust

Barbara Says:

Being able to trust and being trustworthy are markers
of a strong relationship.

*S*he *S*aid: He doesn't follow through and do the things he promises he will do. If I can't trust him with small things like taking out the garbage, how can I trust him with big issues?

I *S*aid: Trust is a small word but a big request.

There are simple things that we need to trust our spouses or partners to do. We need to trust them to take the dog out, feed the cat, put the kids to bed, or get the car washed when they say they will. These are everyday concerns we count on to be done. On a larger scale, we need to trust our spouses to cherish and uphold the vows taken on our wedding day. Whether the issue is small or large, we need to know that we can count on our partner's words and actions without hesitation or worry.

How we define trust makes all the difference in how trusting we behave. When it comes to building trust in a marriage, developing a "trust contract" can help both partners clearly define parameters for their relationship.

Begin the process by writing down behaviors and actions important to each of you in order to trust the other. From that point, together create your personal "trust contract"— a paragraph or two stating your mutual intentions toward creating a partnership filled with trust and support.

In the beginning, you may need to refer to your trust contract often to make sure you are in agreement and following the parameters and guidelines you created together. Keeping your contract at the forefront of your marriage, and committing to it daily, will contribute to building a relationship that will last a lifetime.

While building and maintaining trust may sound like an easy task, in reality, lack of trust causes a significant amount of marital conflict. It is one of the hardest obstacles to overcome when it threatens a relationship. Once trust is lost, rebuilding is a lengthy process, without guarantees for success. For this reason, being able to trust and being trustworthy are two essential traits a strong relationship requires of a couple.

He *said*: I don't know why she makes such a big deal out of whether or not I remember to do the small errands she asks me to do on my way home from work. I can go back out and do them, but she makes me feel like I forgot something major.

I *said*: While it is one of the most important components in any relationship, trust can mean different things to different people, which is where things sometimes get confusing.

In simple terms, trust may mean when you say you will be home by 5:00 p.m., you will actually *be home* by 5:00 p.m.; or when you say you'll do errands on the way home from work, you actually *do them* on the way home from work. It may mean when you call your partner and ask them to take out the casserole for the night's dinner, he/she actually *does it*. It may mean counting on your partner to meet you for an appointment at the time agreed upon. And on a deeper level, trust means you and your spouse or partner are there for each other and have no secrets.

So why is trust on all levels so monumental in a relationship? Because it is the hallmark of being present and in touch with yourself and how the things you say and do impact your relationship.

Trust means creating a sense of comfort and peace, assuring you will not hurt each other intentionally, and making sure that you care about the things that are important to your partner, even if they may seem menial to you. It is also that special quality of vulnerability that allows people to become close to each other.

When an environment of trust exists in a relationship, it also allows for unintentional mistakes in a nonjudgmental environment, along with apologies and forgiveness. It is one of the most necessary and critical components that winds through all the phases and facets of a lasting relationship; without trust, there can be no true relationship.

She Said: This is not what I expected from life. I keep trying to hold on to and create the dream of what I thought life would be, but it just keeps getting farther and farther away from me.

I Said: "We must be willing to let go of the life we have planned, so as to have the life that is waiting for us."

~ E.M. Forster

How much do you try to control your life? How much do you try to plan for the future and create goals for yourself without seeing the possibilities of living in the present? Do you have difficulty trusting the moment?

Sometimes we all look forward or backward and lose sight of what is happening in the here and now. Yet we need to learn to let life happen while watching for the daily miracles coming our way, without questioning why or how we are blessed with them. We need to trust the process of life, understand what our choices are creating for us, and let go of the bargaining and manipulating we so often try to do.

Trust and embrace the life waiting for you and be open to what it brings. Life will be far more satisfying if you are ready and willing to accept new and exciting opportunities that are just around the corner.

Don't create happiness roadblocks for yourself; instead, learn to navigate obstacles and turn them into meaningful challenges. Happiness can be cultivated and is already budding inside each of us.

Learn to explore and turn problems into possibilities, which just might lead to contentment and fulfillment. You are your choices, so let today be the first day you trust yourself to make really good ones.

He Said: My wife travels a lot for her job. It's hard to keep my attention focused on our relationship when she's gone so often. How can I trust that she still feels the same way when we're apart so much?

I Said: "And ever has it been known that love knows not its own depth until the hour of separation."

~ Khalil Gibran

How do you keep your relationship in the present when your spouse or significant other is not physically with you? Is it possible to maintain the same level of trust, love, and acceptance when you don't have much "together" time?

The answer is, "Yes!" True, it takes substantial internal work by each partner to keep feelings alive and current when any kind of distance is involved. Unfortunately, left unchecked, thoughts can sometimes turn into actions and become problematic when a spouse or partner becomes needy, unsure of the relationship, or filled with mistrust because of the physical distance involved.

Good news, with the technology in our world today, staying connected, even from a distance, is possible and doable. With cell phones, emails, texting, messaging, and even video conferencing via Skype, couples can still share special times, encouraging words, love notes, and updates on their days and experiences—from hundreds and even thousands of miles away.

Any kind of connecting and bonding takes time and effort. While being apart may take a different kind of effort, it is still easy to accomplish if you both have the desire and intention to do so. Trust is established by being there for each other and meeting each other's needs. And clear, honest communication can help you each stay in tune with the other to help bridge the gap that a physical separation creates.

She Said: If he still thinks about the other woman, how can I trust him when he says he loves me and wants to be married to me? I have trouble with that.

I Said: Recently, I counseled a couple suffering through infidelity but committed to staying in their marriage and making it better. The spouse, trying to forgive, was having trouble learning to trust again, which was no small task.

Because the couple wanted to save and rebuild their marriage, we talked about prioritizing needs and the rebuilding process necessary to do so. One of the first and most important steps the unfaithful spouse needed to take was to apologize and answer relevant questions pertaining to the affair. When an affair and the feelings around it remain a secret, it is impossible to begin to regain trust from the other partner.

The offending partner must also totally separate himself/ herself from the affair and the person with whom he or she had the affair, because saving a marriage after infidelity requires complete dedication and attention. If his or her thoughts wander to the person with whom he or she was unfaithful, his or her attention is not on the relationship. The offender must take responsibility for the choices he or she made that created the affair, as well as the choices he or she is now making.

Both partners must recognize and address the threats to their relationship and attempt to meet each other's needs as they are now identified; this will take an immense amount of communication on all levels. Each must also be willing to express empathy for the other and accept responsibility for their part in the "marital mistake."

An affair does not have to be a deal breaker in a marriage, but the repair process can sometimes be long and arduous because repairing trust that was so grievously broken is no small task. Constructing a trust contract where each partner's intentions around rebuilding and maintaining trust are put into words can help ensure there is a clear path to follow and there are no hidden expectations.

Interestingly enough, an affair can sometimes be the very thing that strengthens a marriage bond and facilitates a more intimate relationship in the future. This happens because the level of communication and interaction required to overcome the immense breakdown of trust is intensified in efforts by both partners.

He Said: I've never considered that I have any say so
or control in how I feel, let alone being able to trust
my ability to create my life. That's not what I was taught as
a child, and that certainly is not the way I've lived
until now.

I Said: In his book *Your Erroneous Zones,* Dr. Wayne
Dyer tells us, "You are the sum total of your choices."

I also believe in making choices a personal responsibility in
creating one's own happiness and quality of life. Looking at
past choices we've made, and recognizing how they affected
our life's path, can be a guide to making better choices in
the future.

When you get up each morning, you can trust you have
the choice to be positive or negative. From there your day
unfolds. Being happy is something that can be learned and
is well worth the effort. Fostering positive feelings helps
your immune system function better by keeping toxins
away and raising endorphins (www.heartmath.org/free-ser-
vices/solutions-for-stress/solutions-immune-system.html).

Before jumping out of bed each morning, try some of these
simple ways to put yourself into a positive frame of mind
to help set the rhythm for the rest of your day:

- Give yourself the gift of waking up to music instead of an alarm blaring in your ear.

- Listen to the sounds around you. Can you hear birds singing, your children playing, a peaceful quiet?

- Take a few minutes to stretch and allow your body to fully wake up before you hit the ground running.

- Just smile . . . it's really hard to feel negative when we smile.

- List three things for which you are grateful.

- If you can't find three things, just say "thank you" to the universe anyway.

Taking charge of your behavior patterns and trusting that you have the power to do so is a great way to create a more fulfilling, healthier life.

She Said: He accuses me of trying to control everything when all I'm doing is trying to keep things in order. If I didn't, our life would quickly turn into a chaotic mess!

I Said: Many of us have control issues of which we are often unaware. When others choose to point out this "character flaw" to us, the revelation usually comes as a surprise. Trying to control people and events is actually an exercise in futility; the need to control often creates strain in a relationship. The desire to control our worlds is usually the result of not trusting ourselves, our partners, our children, or even life itself.

The truth is we cannot control anyone but ourselves, and we often have trouble doing that. Yet when we can trust the process of life and let go of our need to exercise control, we will feel liberated and open to realizing truths that will make our relationships so much more genuine. When we let things happen the way they are going to happen anyway, we get the real picture. In other words, we are accepting others and situations as they are.

When the need to control flies out the window, feelings are allowed to flow continuously and behavior becomes based on the here and now. By letting go, we may not have it our way all the time, but when each partner is allowed to be exactly

who they are, a feeling of acceptance is created. Each will
know they are loved and cared about with utmost certainty.

Yes, vulnerability creeps in when control is eliminated,
but vulnerability is what allows and fosters intimacy in a
relationship. It allows us to accept our spouse or partner for
what and whom he or she is without our need to change or
control them. It's important to trust that life will not fall
apart if you step away from attempting to be the master of
your universe.

Dr. James McCormick, a good friend and former pastor
in north Georgia, wrote in his book *Marriage is for
Adults*, "The person who is never needy or vulnerable will
always keep us at arm's length, and communication will
be difficult if not impossible. My guess is that arrogance,
pride, stubbornness, dogmatism, and pettiness have ruined
far more marriages than adultery ever did."

Let go of your need to control along with the negative
emotions that may be lurking behind your control issues.
Trust that your life will most likely unfold the same way
whether you try to exercise control or not. Why not just
relax and go with the flow? Your life and relationships
could become much more enjoyable if you do.

He Said: At the beginning of each year, I think about the coming year and making my relationship and life better than it has been. But by the time January 3 is here, I've given up on the idea.

I Said: Most of us talk about making changes in our lives, especially around the beginning of a new year. We talk the talk yet fail to walk the walk. What happens to our thoughts of change and doing things differently? Why do so many resolutions quickly fizzle away?

By definition, a resolution is a determination to do something new, an attempt to improve a behavior or change our lives in some way. In order to do these things, we must trust we have the ability to make changes, and, quite frankly, many of us don't have that trust. The man quoted above is a good example; he simply gave up on the idea of change instead of trusting he had the power to: 1) transform his life, 2) change the way he reacts in his relationship, or 3) adjust the way he views the situation.

True, bettering a marriage or relationship takes two people to make it happen, but one person can be the catalyst for the change. Whether the change requires better communication, developing intimacy, taking time to share loving experiences, or even seeking out the help of a therapist, one partner can start by making new choices within the relationship.

The very first step toward change is to know and then accept that all your simple daily choices will ultimately affect everything happening in your life, and then recognizing that you may have to make new choices to lead you to the results you want. Looking inward to your core beliefs and strengths, as well as visualizing your goals and trusting that you have the ability to create change, will help move you along in this process.

She Said: I no longer trust my choices in men. I have repressed feelings of hurt and anger from my divorce and don't want to go through that again.

I Said: "Becoming a free and healthy person involves learning to think differently. Once you can change your thoughts, your new feelings will begin to emerge, and you will have taken the first step on the road to your personal freedom."

~ Dr. Wayne Dyer, *Your Erroneous Zones*

When we've made choices in the past that have resulted in experiences of pain, it is natural not to trust our own decisions. We have to keep in mind we each have the power to make a different choice at any time. Perhaps this woman did make "bad choices" in men, but she also chose to get out of those relationships. A good, healthy life and relationship begins with trusting yourself to create the best life imaginable for you.

Imagine waking up each morning and, before even getting out of bed, deciding exactly what kind of day you will have, all on your own. You don't need to ask anyone, you don't need to be concerned about what others think, and you especially don't need to feel dependent on anyone but yourself to make the day a positive one. You are totally in control about how *you* will choose to feel for the rest of the day. If during the day you encounter an experience because of a choice you made, you can—then and there—make a different choice. It's important to trust your ability to learn from your experiences and make better choices because of them.

Remember, feelings come from thoughts. Trust the process by putting, even forcing, good thoughts into your mind; good feelings will follow.

Try these simple techniques to help you create good feelings:

- Take time to become aware of what you are thinking.

- If you have a thought that is negative, turn it into a positive. For example, if you think: "I could never___." Change that to: "I can do anything I decide to put my time and energy into doing."

- Be careful of the words you choose. Instead of using the words problem, difficult, or burden, try switching to words like opportunity, challenge, growth, and experience.

- Develop an "attitude of gratitude" and think about what's good in your life instead of what isn't.

Remember, thoughts create feelings, feelings create actions, and actions create our lives. If the choice were yours each moment of the day, why would you choose to be anything but happy? You've got the power of choice—trust that concept and leave your "bad choices" in the past as you move forward with good, healthy choices for your future.

He Said: I stopped feeling connected in my marriage many years ago, but I just don't trust myself to make the right decision about staying or leaving, so I just stay stuck.

I Said: This client was in a marriage where he and his spouse had grown apart over the last few years. Yet he had only positive things to say about his wife. His complaint was he didn't feel they had much in common anymore, and he didn't want to spend the rest of his life feeling so disconnected.

He was stuck because he didn't trust his ability to make the right decision to stay or go. Additionally, he didn't trust his spouse and wasn't sure their marriage could be rebuilt even if effort was put into it. He hadn't reached out to communicate his feelings. In other words, he hadn't done anything about what he was feeling . . . one way or the other. As the saying goes, "Nothing changes, until something changes."

In essence, staying on the fence in any situation keeps people stuck and doesn't allow for growth and change. For change to occur, it is necessary to fully examine all possibilities and contingencies, and then trust yourself that you can either change the situation you're in or create a new situation. Trusting that ability can actually allow the situation to be improved, or it will affect a change of course.

One of my professors at Georgia State University once said, "Make a decision and make it the right one."

Easier said than done perhaps, but the alternative of staying stuck in a less than satisfying circumstance is not perfect either. Trust yourself that you have what it takes to create a life that is satisfying for you and know you have what it takes to make choices and take the steps required.

Forgiveness

Barbara Says:

Look to forgive both the large and small hurts
caused by another.

*S*he *S*aid: How can I forgive him when I can't yet forget what he's done?

I *S*aid: Recently, Lifetime Movie Network ran a true-life drama titled *Amish Grace*. It is an exceptionally powerful film with a strong message of forgiveness.

The story was linked to a unique cultural religious group, the Pennsylvania Amish. In 2006, while attending school, six Amish children were murdered by Charles Carl Roberts. A number of children were released from the school, but the others held hostage were trussed and terrorized before they were shot.

Although the Amish community grieved deeply, shortly after the massacre, one of the murdered children's grandfather said, "We must not think evil of this man."

The gentle community went to comfort the killer's family to ease the grief, shame, and despair they were surely feeling at their loss.

Such a strong message of forgiveness the actions of the Amish people spoke that day!

One line in the movie was particularly meaningful to me. It went something like this, "Forgiving doesn't mean forgetting, and it doesn't mean pardoning. But if we hold onto our anger and resentment, it is only ourselves who are being punished. When we open our hearts to forgiveness, darkness vanishes and evil is no more."

Those words resonate strongly in an intimate relationship. It's important to ask yourself if it is more important to hold on to anger and resentment after being hurt, or if it is better to move forward with an open, forgiving heart so the negativity, stress, and emotional separation felt between you and your partner can be eliminated.

Forgiveness, like all other behaviors in life, is a choice.

He Said: I feel angry with her all the time—for things she's done in the past and even for little things she does now, which shouldn't be any big deal; but they are, because I can't seem to let go of the pain.

I Said: From the forgiver's standpoint, offering forgiveness enables releasing the feelings keeping him or her stuck in a deepening pit of anger, resentment, and hurt. But, it doesn't excuse behavior, and it doesn't mean quickly and easily trusting the person who caused the hurt and pain.

It does mean setting healthy boundaries with the person who did the wounding, as well as working through the emotions triggered by his or her hurtful behavior. It doesn't mean automatically forgetting what was done. What it does do is allow the person forgiving to reach out and begin a process of reconciliation.

If you have a nagging sense of anger, hurt, or resentment from choices your partner has made in the past or behaviors he or she has exhibited toward you, choosing to forgive him or her will help *you* find peace. While your choice to forgive will help the offending person feel safe to step back into a relationship with you, extending forgiveness will have the biggest impact on your own life because you will then choose to let go of negative thoughts and emotions that have been filling your mind and your heart.

What you think and what you feel are your choices. If you are holding on to old hurts and resentments, you are choosing not to move forward and will learn nothing from the negative experiences. You will not be able to move on to better times.

*S*he *S*aid: Something will happen at work or on the drive home, and then he becomes angry and hard to get along with all night, and sometimes even into the next day. I just want him to "get over it" and move on.

I *S*aid: In the hustle and bustle of everyday life, we sometimes experience others' unpleasant behaviors. Ugly acts might be as mundane as somebody cutting in line at Starbucks, or it might be something as serious as the infidelity of a spouse. One thing is for sure, when upsetting behaviors happen, it is easy to harbor feelings of anger, bitterness, hostility, and hatred, and we bring those feelings into every facet of our life, often harming ourselves and those we love the most.

Check Google. Forgiveness is a hot research topic with thousands of clinical studies examining the process of forgiving. Research shows the act of pardoning has benefits for the one taking the action. These benefits include the reduction of stress when forgiveness occurs, as well as the ability to maintain or build a stronger relationship. By forgiving others for actions and behaviors, both big and small, personal isolation is diminished and the hurt alienating us from others dissipates. Studies abound showing those who have strong relationships are healthier than loners who are apt to shed relationships when they hold a grudge.

Let go of the myriad of hurts and offenses that occur throughout your days and choose to forgive even the "big" offenses committed by those you love the most. Forgiving doesn't imply excusing, nor does it forgo justice. Instead, the benefit of exoneration is found in the relief of personal suffering; it has little to do with condoning negative actions of others.

You can choose to forgive and make the decision to reconcile with the perpetrator, or you can internally accept the wrongdoing. Whether you choose decisional or emotional forgiveness, the benefit will be the same—a healthy alternative to anger, hostility, or hatred.

So, just for today, try taking good care of yourself and see if you can forgive just one person you feel mistreated you. Hopefully, it will become a habit, and you will eventually embark on a smarter path to better mental health. Not only will your life become happier, but you will also be more pleasant to be around, which can only have a positive impact on your personal relationships.

He said: We've been married for six years and overall it's been good, but in the back of my mind, I remember how she broke up with me just months before we were supposed to get married. We worked it all out, but those memories still hurt.

I said: We all have memories—some happy, some sad—and often we keep our happy, cherished memories in scrapbooks or photo albums. Yet in our heart's memory box, we frequently lock away hurt feelings and wrongs committed against us, even from as long ago as our childhood. Many people even report sleepless nights spent recounting unresolved hurts that happened decades before.

Perhaps you are someone who often says, "I forgave him (or her) for what he (or she) did, but I'll never forget it." Unfortunately, if that is your approach to life and forgiveness, emotional garbage will always clutter your head and heart because you are holding on to the memories of a painful experience. Instead, you have the ability to choose to accept that "it is what it is" and then make healthy choices around what thoughts you let into your mind and what memories you hold in your heart.

People make mistakes every day, especially in a long-term relationship. Keeping a tally of mistakes and hurts will only weigh down the relationship and it does not liberate either partner.

She Said: How can I not be angry? He's done some things in the past that have hurt me. Maybe they aren't huge in someone else's eyes, but for me they're painful. He says he's sorry, but I feel resentful that I had to go through those experiences in the first place.

I Said: In her book, *The Magic of Forgiveness*, Dr. Tian Dayton addresses forgiveness as a process. Dayton wrote her book as a guide for women in their middle years to recognize and use the power of forgiveness to heal past wounds and resentments.

She cites five stages in the forgiving process:

1. Waking up—Looking at the reality of the situation along with any blocks to forgiveness that may exist or fears that could be getting in the way

2. Dealing with anger and resentment—Recognizing if your anger is past or present, along with learning how to manage your anger

3. Hurt and sadness—Feeling your feelings

4. Acceptance, integration, and letting go—Coming to terms with the hurt and releasing the past

5. Reorganization and reinvestment—
    Recreating your life with a focus on things
    like a spiritual belief system, good values,
    intimacy, and developing an attitude of
    gratitude and appreciation

Whether it is a small or large action we are forgiving, it is a process to travel from hurt to peace, but it is a worthwhile path to follow. When we forgive someone, we are led to a new emotional connection, perhaps more intense than what was experienced in the past. This new connection allows for vulnerability because we feel safe, which in turn creates emotional freedom.

He *said*: When I do something that hurts her, I say
I'm sorry over and over again, but it just doesn't seem
to be enough.

I *said*: How often do we hurt the ones we love?

Sometimes we hurt others unintentionally, innocently, and
regretfully. Sometimes we hurt others purposefully.

Unfortunately, we can't take back hurtful words or
behaviors. Once words have been said or actions are done,
they are "out there" for eternity, no matter how much we
regret our unintentional or intentional cruelty.

So how can we correct our words or actions? We can begin
by apologizing, being sincere with our words of promise
for new beginnings in the relationship. It's also important
to affirm the hurt we have caused and let loved ones know
we made a terrible mistake with what we said or did.
Affirming feelings on both sides and allowing responses to
flow are the keys to a meaningful apology.

An apology without the willingness to hear and accept the
feelings of the ones we've hurt is empty and meaningless.
Our loved ones need to know we are willing to listen
to their pain and sadness, and affirm and accept our

responsibility for causing them to suffer. Interestingly enough, apologizing to another is the first step to forgiving ourselves for our unacceptable behaviors.

It is also important that an apology is followed by a change in behavior. If you say, "I'm sorry" yet continue to exhibit the same behaviors as before, your words become hollow. If your apology doesn't seem to be enough, look at the way you made the apology and your behaviors following it.

She Said: I walk around with a knot in my stomach most of the time. I know it's because I can't forgive him for the stupid way he handled a situation with his family, but he really hurt me!

I Said: If you can't forgive your partner for the hurt they have caused, do it for you. Medical studies, including those done at the Mayo Clinic, have confirmed when you find it in your heart to forgive, your body will react by lowering your blood pressure, strengthening your immune system, decreasing your anxiety and depression, improving your sleep, building your self-esteem, reducing your stress, and increasing your energy (www.mayoclinic.com/health/ forgiveness/MH00131). What's not to like about that?

We all know there are things we need to do to maintain a good quality of life. In fact, the media bombards us with commercials and advertisements about vitamins, herbs, and antioxidants while encouraging us to exercise to keep in shape and free from disease.

The focus is to prevent stress from taking its toll on our bodies by weakening our immune system, which could lead to illness. We are reminded to incorporate food, supplements, and activities into our lifestyle to reduce stress and promote wellness.

But all the vitamins and push-ups in the world won't help a hurting heart. Try forgiving those who have hurt you, intentionally or unintentionally. This will forge a sense of well-being, contentment, and peace to promote your own good health.

So, what's keeping you from forgiving? Make the process about taking care of yourself. There's a lot to be gained!

He Said: Maybe it's me . . . I don't know. She says I'm a pessimist but I've always thought of myself as a realist.

I Said: "Practice being optimistic," writes Dr. Richard Blue in his book, *Dr. Blue's Guide to Making Relationships Work*. He goes on to say, "Ask yourself to think about three positive events that have happened in your relationship. Do this on a weekly basis. Challenge your negative thinking by focusing on the positives of each situation. Remember to seek out and enjoy positive experiences."

It is easy to complain about what is not going right in our lives, or to hold onto angers or resentment, but that won't lead to better choices. While hurt and pain happen in a relationship, there are also things that occur each day that we can be thankful for, and it is focusing on these things that will make forgiveness achievable and life much more enjoyable.

Focusing on what we have invested in and harvested is far more beneficial than counting deficits or agonizing over what we feel we are missing. Using positive energy to move forward can give past hurts or disappointments a charge to spark change. It's never too late to make something better, or at least view it in a different way.

Let go of what happened in the past and concentrate on what is happening now. Why don't you take a moment and think of three positive events that you have to be thankful for in your relationship?

She Said: I didn't "sign on" for all of this when I said I'd marry him. I feel like I've been sold a bill of goods. How can I forgive him for that?

I Said: There will be situations in every life and relationship that aren't expected and that we didn't "sign on" for. Life isn't always easy, predictable, or even fair. But in every circumstance, we have the ability to make life better for ourselves and for those we love with the choices we make. But if we're so caught up in being angry with our partner because life isn't unfolding the way we expected, we cheat ourselves out of the chance for happiness. Life happens, and we don't always have control over what happens. The good news is, we do have control over the choices we make surrounding circumstances. There is a saying that goes something like this: "Life is 10 percent about what happens to us, and 90 percent about what we do with it."

Instead of spending your time and energy harboring anger or resentment because life isn't what you expected, look at the things in your life that are good. Begin by asking yourself these five questions:

1. What can I be thankful for today?

2. What can I enjoy today?

3. What can I be satisfied about today?

4. What is better in my life than I ever
    expected it to be?

5. What blessings do I have that I haven't
    seen because I've been holding on to old
    perceptions of what I thought my life would
    be?

Living in the past is a waste of energy and a waste of your
life source. Remember, we only have so many days on this
Earth. Do you really want to spend your days holding a
grudge against your loved one because life isn't exactly what
you expected?

Intimacy

Barbara Says:

In order to be intimate, one must be able to be vulnerable.

He Said: I have this intimacy issue because I am not able to open up to others easily, and it is affecting my relationship with my partner.

I Said: Sometimes the intimacy problems we have in our relationships start with a personal issue one of the partners is experiencing. If one is unable to feel comfortable releasing and opening to the other, intimacy will be difficult to achieve.

If the intimacy in your relationship is not what you want it to be, a good place to start is examining your attitudes about interacting with others and perhaps even how you relate to life itself.

During one session, I was talking with a client and commented on her positive attitude. She said she was one of those people lucky enough to view a glass as half full.

Then she added, "And I also know the waiter will be filling my glass again."

Wow, I thought, what a way to live a life! If we all could harness that attitude, the quality of our days would be greatly increased.

When it comes to marriage or an intimate relationship, it's always best to focus on the good aspects to show the way up instead of the way down. How you view the events and experiences affecting your relationship reveals much about how you will handle difficulties, challenges, or even the wonderful times. Changing or adjusting your attitude can make all the difference in the world.

Do you think of your relationship in terms of the positive force it brings to your life? Or do you dwell on all that is missing? Are you afraid to open up to others and accept the possibility of vulnerability, or do you embrace what life throws your way with gusto and excitement?

It's all a matter of perspective, and the good news is, you get to choose yours.

*S*he *S*aid: When we were first together, we made time for each other. Now there seems to be time for everything else except us.

I *S*aid: There are many ways to define love and intimacy, and many interpretations for each definition. One of the definitions I recently came across is this very short and simple phrase: "Love is time spent."

It may be a brief sentiment, but it is indeed one of the most profound, because love and intimacy are about getting to know each other, and that happens by spending time together in a variety of situations.

Time is the most precious commodity we have, and when we choose to share any of our moments with someone else, we are giving the most treasured gift we have to offer. And yet, our hours do not have a price tag attached to them.

We often spend much thought and energy on giving each other "things" for special occasions, but one of the greatest ways to express how much you love someone is to spend time with them. Intimacy is developed when we give each other the gift of time spent together, and that is one gift that will *never* be returned. Time spent will continue to reap benefits for both partners for years to come, but one of the greatest ways to express how much you love someone is to spend time with them. And, as a result, intimacy will develop, and that is a gift that will never be returned. The more time a couple spends together, the more benefits they will reap.

Look at the days and weeks in front of you. How much time have you allocated for being with each other? Don't expect that it "will just happen," because life can often get in the way and the best of intentions don't manifest into actions. So plan a walk, a date, a time to talk, or an evening curled up watching a favorite old movie together. Whatever it is that the two of you like to do together, make sure to reserve time in your schedule for just the two of you. Give each other the most precious gift you can give . . . the gift of yourself and your time.

He *S*aid: She knows how I feel about her. I don't think flowers or a little note is going to make that big a difference. That's what people do before they have a strong relationship together. Once you have it, it's just there but my wife doesn't seem to feel the same way.

I *S*aid: Suppose you just finished building a new house. You made it just the way you wanted it, paid close attention to detail, and you're finally ready to move in. Everything is perfect. So you move in, settle down, and are exceptionally happy with everything.

But five years later, the luster seems to be gone—floors are scratched, paint is fading, carpets are worn, and the pipes leak. Well, what did you expect? Without continuing attention and frequent maintenance, nothing stays perfect for long.

Move on to your marriage. You had a fabulous courtship, beautiful wedding, and exciting honeymoon. Everything was perfect, and you know you found the partner of your dreams. Fast-forward five years. Is the perfection gone?

Intimacy is about giving ongoing attention and maintenance to your relationship, much the way you would do for anything you love. As years pass, you may notice areas in your relationship that need improvement.

The tender feelings you experienced during dating, your wedding, and honeymoon often fade into only memories. Life has moved on, as it always does, and if you haven't done much to maintain what you had, intimacy and feelings of connection are probably just distant memories as well.

As with a house, your relationship requires continuing attention. It requires a daily commitment to keep it the main priority for both of you, or it too will lose its luster.

I've created a commitment agreement that goes like this: "I agree to keep my marriage as my utmost priority and work on it every day. I will not allow any cause to be a reason to forget my agreement. It is my hope that my everlasting love for you, along with this agreement, will help me achieve the gift of a lifetime—a lasting marriage."

Begin to think about ways to maintain your marriage or relationship. List things you could do on a daily basis to make it happen. By continuing to put time and energy into your relationship, you will continue to build and maintain an intimate connection that will bring continued happiness and contentment to both of you.

*∫*he *∫*aid: Our life has become all about work, the kids, and keeping the mortgage paid. I'm not sure I even remember what it feels like to be passionate and playful anymore.

I *∫*aid: Is your relationship stagnant? Is it lacking excitement and passion? Is lovemaking fast becoming just another thing on your to-do list, if it's on the list at all? If you answered, "Yes," to any of these questions, here is the antidote—date your spouse!

Remember the tingling anticipation you felt getting ready for a date with your lover? Try to create that feeling again with new dating experiences. Yes, it can be done!

As a starting point, think where you went and what you liked to do when you were dating. Going back in time to revisit old haunts is wonderful, but also discover new places and conversations to keep things interesting, exciting, fresh, and fun.

Plan fun, romantic, and even old-fashioned budget dates and follow these six ground rules to guarantee a "high wow" connection with your partner:

1.   Make dating a habit for creating time to rediscover and focus on each other.

2. Think outside the box for dating ideas. Visiting an amusement park, museum, art show, or even walking in the park are old standbys. Why not take a class, join a book club, get massaged, or find a new hobby . . . together.

3. It's really important to plan talking points. Stay away from discussing finances, work, kids, or household problems. Get to know each other all over again without distractions.

4. It goes without saying, leave the kids at home!

5. Add a little spice, mystery, and something totally unexpected to your date. This might be a great time to leave your underwear at home.

6. HAVE FUN, and love the one you're with!

Intimacy is about shared experiences, laughter, and connection. It's up to the two of you to create those moments and opportunities together.

He Said: We know what we need to do, but we just need to execute it. We need to make the time for our marriage.

I Said: In the beginning of this book, I provided a sample relationship maintenance agreement to use as a guide and focus to keep your relationship in the forefront of your thoughts and behaviors. Keeping your relationship as your utmost priority and putting time and energy into it (maintaining it) is an essential part of creating intimacy with your partner. It will also energize you personally and present new chapters for individual growth.

We take care of our cars with scheduled maintenance, including oil changes, tire rotations, and everything else critical to keep our vehicles running well. So why not look at our relationships as needing required maintenance, too? Unlike a car, a relationship doesn't cost much to maintain, just time, patience, and thoughtfulness.

Why not plan a 30-day checkup at the end of every month to ensure that you and your partner are still on the same page? If things need readjusting, modify your agreement. Then do something special and fun together to celebrate how well you're doing.

The benefit of consciously maintaining your relationship will allow you to achieve a connection that will become more meaningful and intimate.

*S*he *S*aid: My best friend was telling me about some of the romantic things she does for her husband. We don't do a lot of that in our relationship. Is it important?

I *S*aid: Receiving attention from the one you love is a shared need in any relationship. We often think of attention as a female need and assume men don't need or want attention as much; but, in reality, men also love having attention paid to them by their special someone.

How much attention do you and your partner give to the little things you can do for and with each other? Do you still hold hands in the movies? How about when you are taking a walk? Do you ever gently touch the cheek of your partner? Or bring them a special treat you know they'll love? These little affectionate gestures are signs of paying attention to the special person you are spending your life with.

If you're not sure what affectionate gestures your partner would enjoy, ask him or her. Or, try different things and see how they respond. It is often the little things that we do for each other that make the biggest difference in the connection we have. And the memories of the small thoughtful things we do frequently last for a lifetime. Little things mean a lot, especially when they linger as memories.

In fact, I've talked with many people who are widowed,

and most say it is the little signs of affection from their spouse they miss the most. One widow sighed as she recounted sitting on the lawn with her husband on a summer night to enjoy the stars. She now believes her late husband is one of those very stars and is watching over her, with a twinkle in his eye no less!

Another widow misses her husband bringing her coffee and the newspaper each morning. Yet another widow remembers her husband picking a bouquet of flowers for her from their yard. One widower misses his wife placing freshly ironed handkerchiefs in his bureau drawer and baking a chocolate cake each month, just for him.

It is always the sweet, affectionate behaviors that leave lasting marks in one's memory. Getting to know your partner and the affectionate gestures they appreciate will allow you both to grow the intimacy you crave.

He Said: Any intimacy we once had is gone, but I still stay in the relationship, and I don't know why.

I Said: We all love, absolutely love, the exhilarating sense of excitement a new relationship brings to our lives. Even Kodak captured love's thrill in their commercial picturing a man and a woman running through the fields in slow motion, ready to fall into each other's arms with wild abandon.

Those first months of found love really bring out the best in us, and we fervently promise our love will never fade. As a couple, we *will* be different!

Well, then life happens.

Children are born, careers change, moves are made, in-laws fight, teens leave the nest, pounds are gained, and wrinkles appear in the most unattractive places. After a round of years, love and life often become a routine series of obligations and drills until one morning, over the fourth cup of black coffee at the kitchen counter, tears roll and we ask, "Is this all there is?"

But, what does "all" really mean? Intimacy as defined by commercials, television shows, and movies brings visions of a caress or longing glance in the early throes of passion.

Yet if we confine ourselves to that definition, we can often miss the deeper stages of intimacy that slowly morph into something quite different as life and love experiences add chapters to our lives.

In the Bing dictionary, a "sexual connection" is the last definition given for "intimacy." The words and phrases "close relationship, quiet atmosphere, detailed knowledge, private utterance or action, understanding, confidence, caring, tenderness, seclusion, informality, friendliness, and warmth" are more often used to describe the sense of intimacy.

In real life, there is certain peace and sexiness, too, that comes from feeling safe and comfortable with the one you love. Rolling your eyes at your partner when Uncle Harry revs up his chicken dance for the umpteenth time brings a sense of closeness and connection to you both, if not a shared chuckle.

Intimacy is all about sharing the day-to-day joys, hassles, pains, and promises we weave together to pattern our relationships. The sexual connection is wonderful, too, no mistake about it. But, what one thing would you really miss the most if your love fell off the face of the earth tonight?

One sweet little old lady answered, "First, I'd miss the way my husband always made me feel, and then I'd miss the dent he made sitting in his favorite chair!" That's tough to beat!

If you think the intimacy in your relationship is gone, you might want to just look again. Perhaps it isn't gone. It has simply changed forms, and you haven't been looking in the right places.

She Said: I just can't seem to enjoy sex the way he wants me to. He is focusing on it 24/7 and I am trying to accommodate him, but it is getting tough.

I Said: How we say it . . . how we do it . . . how we show it . . . how we feel it.

The sexual experience that partners share is always important, although it is often a difficult subject for couples to discuss. In my counseling practice, I often hear sex is either absent, withheld, or is not a shared desire.

There is something wonderful about relating to each other through intensely intimate sexual contact. Making love with your partner without embarrassment, shyness, or fear of being vulnerable releases so much for us. Being able to talk about what pleasures us or exploring triggers for arousal pushes through limits of vulnerability.

In his book, *Equality: The Quest for the Happy Marriage,* author Tim Kellis makes this profound statement, "The difference between sex and intimacy is sex is when you are doing it for your pleasure while intimacy is when you are doing it for your partner's pleasure."

Which is it for you? Is sex primarily about getting your physical needs met, or is it about caring for your partner so their sexual desires are fulfilled? Are you so caught up in your internal sexual fantasies that you ignore the sexual needs or interests of your partner?

If one partner's sexual appetite or interest isn't as strong as the other's, maybe it's time for you as a couple to leave your comfort zone and talk about what each wants and needs in the bedroom. Couples often find they grow closer when they risk venturing into new sexual territory and concentrate on pleasing each other instead of just having their own needs met.

A new sexual experience can be a powerful stimulus to ignite passion, while also creating feelings of quiet intimacy. Interestingly enough, when desires mesh and weave into a crescendo, the sexual experience is intensified for both. Often what happens in the bedroom transfers to other spheres of a life lived together. Sharing a strong sexual bond can make everyday life an adventure.

Romance, passion, and sexual excitement are all ingredients necessary for fostering intimacy, which can only increase as a couple exposes deeper feelings to each other. Do what it takes to make your shared sexual experiences a vital part of the rest of your life together.

He Said: I'm not sure that I know what intimacy really is. I just know that I don't think we have it either in or out of the bedroom.

I Said: "Intimacy is often defined as the ability to reveal all aspects of oneself to another and feel accepted."

~ Richard C. Schwartz

Intimacy is an important aspect of a healthy marriage or long-term relationship. It is also one of the most misunderstood, as most couples think of intimacy exclusively in sexual terms. This is yet another communication breakdown. While sex is certainly a strong component of intimacy, it is only one. True intimacy involves sexual, intellectual, spiritual, and emotional closeness.

When a couple is experiencing sexual intimacy problems, whether it has to do with the infrequency or quality of their sexual interactions, the problem can often be traced back to a lack of intimacy in another area; many times lack of emotional bonding is the culprit.

Intimacy takes on varying characteristics and roles in every relationship, and developing one facet of intimacy can often pilot others. For example, if you were first drawn to your partner for his intellectual prowess, but after a few years repainting the house became more pressing than Proust, try reaching back into your past to rediscover intellectual passions you once enjoyed. A shared literary lecture at your local library can be the catalyst for bonding on many levels, all leading to a sense of emotional reattachment that is the core trait of intimacy. Or if in the beginning you spent hours together just talking and laughing about a variety of subjects, reignite those embers by creating the time and place for uninterrupted conversations.

Intimacy for you and your partner will be different and unique because of who you both are, so try thinking of personalized ways to be intimate with your spouse or partner. Start with the little things and build as assurance grows. Always remember that reconnecting, rebuilding, or simply reinforcing relationships is an ongoing process as life is ever changing. Instead of thinking of this process as work to be done, consider the opportunities it will bring!

She Said: We just don't have the time for each other that we used to have. How can we possibly feel the same way that we did back then?

I Said: One of the biggest misconceptions in life is that the quantity of time spent determines the quality of it. That is far from the truth. If the schedules and obligations of your lives do not allow you the amount of time together that you once had, instead of bemoaning that fact, do something to make the time you do have together time well spent for creating a connection, bond, and intimacy.

As each day dawns, think of exciting ways to create intimate moments for you and your special someone. Let even small amounts of time work for you. Here are a few ideas to get you started:

- Greet the morning by saying to your special someone, "I love you."

- Wear your widest smile to welcome them into the day.

- Say thank you for all the little things your partner does for you.

- Make it a priority to pay one sincere compliment to your partner on a daily b   .

- Spend time together as a couple, if only for a few minutes.

- Find a wonderful thing about your life and share it with your mate.

- Ask what you can do to make your partner's day better or easier.

- Act on things instead of just thinking about them.

When night falls, you're sure to go to bed with a smile on your face, warmth in your heart, and a closer connection with your partner.

He Said: She doesn't seem interested in sex, so it's hard for me to be interested in what she cares about.

I Said: Do you really know whether or not your partner is interested in sex, or are you just assuming and then reacting to your own assumption? Talking about sex in a steamy locker room or over a few hands of bridge is nothing like facing your partner and asking, "Hey, baby, what really turns you on?" Yikes!

We sometimes act quite liberated when discussing sex in public, perhaps wanting to appear worldly, uninhibited, or shocking to our friends. After all, sex talk hasn't been taboo for decades and speaking in generalities to an audience doesn't require we release our *real* secrets.

But, getting to the nitty gritty with your partner can be downright scary, especially if you're really not sure if your fantasies are "acceptable." What if you shock their pants off, literally and figuratively? If you're unsure of their reaction, start off slowly by trying new techniques and watching their response. You might be surprised. Adding some spice to your bedroom and your sexual encounters might generate a reaction and connection that can catapult your level of intimacy to exactly where you want it to be.

Not sure how to start? Here's something that might help.

Search out "intimacy enhancers" on the Internet. You don't have to go to a porn site—many reputable companies sell enhancers or sex toys. Go ahead, let your imagination wander and find a few interesting items to try. Order up! Yes, they do come in plain brown wrappers. Or visit a health and wellness shop; often, you can find Kama Sutra influences on the shelves.

You'll also find plenty of CDs featuring erotic beats to stimulate bedroom antics.

A close sexual connection between partners is a vital part of intimacy in a healthy relationship. Interestingly, it is often one of the more difficult areas for couples to openly discuss with each other. Yet, sometimes by simply stepping outside of the box and bringing some "steamy moments" back into the bedroom, intimacy gets a good foothold and spreads into the other areas of your life as well. If talking about sex with your partner is too uncomfortable to bear, try leaving hints around your bedroom. A glimpse of lace or a sexy magazine can set your bedroom on fire! What a rush of pleasure awaits!

Acceptance

Barbara Says:

Acceptance: We all want and need it, so let's give it.

She Said: I want everything to be equally shared: the kids, the house, and life in general. I don't want to have to ask every time something needs doing. He lives here too; why do I have to be in charge of our entire domestic world?

I Said: Recently, I was talking with a couple about progress made since they began counseling. Both agreed they were doing better. They reported significant improvement communicating with each other. But the wife continued to talk about her need for her husband to take on more family duties and responsibilities. She wanted him to show more initiative. She felt her husband should *know* what needed to be done, and then do it.

Although the wife indicated her spouse was much better at doing what she requested, she thought he still should be more proactive and do things on this own. She said, "He is in a man's world and I am in a woman's world, and they are never going to be the same."

How true!

The differences between men and women are so numerous that author John Gray has written a whole series of books on the subject. And while we can lament and complain about these differences as long as the world exists, they aren't going to change just because we don't like them.

What you can do as a couple is to recognize the differences between the two of you and play to those strengths. If you're better at "being in charge," then that's your strength. Your mate might be better at keeping the cars running, mowing the lawn, budgeting your finances, or simply being a strong support when needed.

We are all different. Fighting those differences is energy wasted, while accepting the other exactly as he or she is will allow your life together to flow smoothly.

He Said: Women need love, and men need respect. It's as simple as that.

I Said: "Love is the ability and willingness to allow those that you care for to be what they choose for themselves without any insistence that they satisfy you."

~ Wayne Dyer

In order to have a successful relationship, couples must accept each other for whom and what they are. This is the essence of both love and respect; there truly is no difference.

The process must start with respecting and loving who each of you are. If you aren't comfortable accepting yourselves, how can you expect someone to return the favor?

Once you cherish your personal uniqueness, it is easier to respect and accept the differences in others. When you appreciate each other's shortcomings, warts and all, you open yourselves to more readily understanding the quirks, faults, and idiosyncrasies of those you love.

It's important to treat lovers as friends, respecting the boundaries of the relationship.

The crux of a solid relationship has nothing to do with changing your partner to suit what you think they should be. Instead, it is about knowing exactly who they are and loving and respecting them because of it.

*S*he *S*aid: I believe that "what you put out is what you get back," and he just can't seem to grasp that concept.

I *S*aid: Ever thought about living your life on a Möbius strip?

According to the *American Heritage Dictionary*, a Möbius strip is a continuous one-sided surface that can be formed from a rectangular strip by rotating one end 180° and attaching it to the other end. This single continuous curve demonstrates that the Möbius strip has only one boundary.

It is quite a concept and goes something like this, "Whatever is inside of us continually flows outward to help form or deform the world—and whatever is outside us continually flows inward to help form or deform our lives." ~ *Finding Your Soul*, Parker J. Palmer.

I became interested in the Möbius concept after asking a client what her goal for counseling was and she answered, "To live my life on the Möbius strip." What an interesting idea!

I do believe that client brought something new into my thought processes, and for that I am thankful. It is a gift when we learn something new from a person, even though we may be the one theoretically helping that person tackle the problem. Look around you for such special situations and see how the people you meet each day can enrich your lives and teach you how to look at things in new and novel ways. Changing your viewpoint can change your world.

When we look at our lives as a continuum of time, the knowledge and insight we gain from interacting with others can flow continuously to affect all we think and do.

He Said: Of course I love her, but sometimes it's really hard for me to like her because we're so different.

I Said: One of the strengths of a healthy relationship is acceptance of the other.

Think about how accepting (or not) you are of your partner or significant other. Even if you think you have this attribute mastered, it never hurts to go through a checklist to make sure you're on track. How you show your acceptance of another might not carry the message you think you are sending.

Here are some tips from my book, *The Gift of a Lifetime: Building a Marriage That Lasts,* to help you learn to accept the pleasures and limitations of your partner:

- Learn not to criticize—Ridiculing your mate for behavior you do not find acceptable will not make the other change. It will only make the problem grow.

- Be a good listener—Sometimes, when a person can talk with his/her partner and feel the other is really interested in hearing about a problem, a resolution can be found.

- Have realistic expectations of your mate and

relationship—It is what it is. Your marriage/
relationship is a work in progress. Accept that
fact. Then let time and love take its course!

It's important to accept the fact that you and your partner
are two individual people, and how you act and react to
life and the many situations that occur will be different.
Neither of you are wrong or right; you are just different.

It is impossible to live a lifetime with someone and always
like every aspect of his or her behavior. Just remember that
during those moments that you don't like that person,
you still love him or her, and then base your behavior and
reactions on that reality.

She Said: The way he thinks is sometimes so bizarre to me! He'll make a comment, and I find myself totally baffled where he came up with that crazy idea!

I Said: A man and woman simply think differently. For this very reason, I often recommend the book, *Men Are From Mars, Women Are From Venus,* by Dr. John Gray, to the couples I counsel. When one partner feels the other may not be living up to their expectations or complying with their requests, it may simply be that the other person has a different perception of the situation.

Along with recognizing the reality of male/female differences, being open to at least listening to your partner's point of view is essential in building a relationship where each of you feels accepted for who you are. When you are both able to express your thoughts and feelings openly and honestly, an atmosphere of love and acceptance will develop.

You may baffle each other with your varying points of view, and you may often wonder where the other "came up with that crazy idea." But a healthy relationship is one where each partner feels safe and comfortable enough to express their ideas, no matter how crazy or "off the wall" they may be.

Being accepted exactly as you are by someone you love is probably one of the most satisfying feelings in the world.

He Said: I wasn't prepared for all the adjusting my children and I would have to do when I married a woman who had children of her own. We had our individual family lifestyles before. But now when our families combined, everything seems to be in turmoil. The dogs are even causing problems!

I Said: During one session, I was talking with a client about marital concerns proving to be disruptive to family life. It was a second marriage for both, and there were blended family issues. The newly formed couple each had two children of varying ages and sexes, and all were trying to adjust to their new life roles together.

Oddly enough, the couple's issues weren't the usual child-centered problems facing blended families. Instead, their worries centered on their dogs learning to accept each other's territory and role within the new family structure.

I had never worked with this type "blending" before, so it was quite refreshing, if not challenging. One of the dogs was simply not adjusting well to the other and was causing significant distress to the family. The disgruntled pooch was exhibiting poor coping skills, such as biting, growling, and other debilitating acts of canine aggression. This couple was certainly distraught. Each loved their animal and wanted to keep them in the family, but they needed peace, too.

Marital therapy was directed at the communication necessary to maintain structure when blending two families, using the welfare of the dogs as a point of reference. Several interventions were suggested giving options for this couple to explore.

Quite a unique approach to blended families, indeed!

Blended family problems are always challenging and require copious amounts of compassion, acceptance, and commitment for resolutions to be successful. Each new family member has a role to play, and they must be clearly defined and assigned.

She Said: It's hard to admit we're having problems in our marriage, let alone looking at what we need to do to fix them.

I Said: I was busily autographing copies of my first book at a signing one day when a couple standing nearby commented they believed all things happened for a reason. They were just passing by the Books-A-Million storefront when it occurred to them to take the time to stop in.

As it turned out, they were having marital problems and seeing a copy of my book, *The Gift of a Lifetime: Building a Marriage That Lasts,* caught their attention.

After they read the headings and browsed the chapters, we chatted for a bit. The couple spotted a special passage in the book that called to them and they eagerly bought a copy.

Because the couple openly accepted the fact that they were having problems and then were willing to take steps to fix the difficulties, their chances for rebuilding a connection and intimacy are extremely good.

Ignorance definitely is not bliss, and things don't go away when ignored. Masking your fears, worries, and anxieties under a pleasant demeanor, or filling your days with mindless activity to avoid dealing with issues, is a façade waiting to crumble.

The first and most crucial step to rebuilding lost intimacy is to recognize, accept, and admit your relationship is not what you both want it to be, but knowing you both have the power to change it. Only then will you be open to experiences and opportunities facilitated by change.

Friendship

Barbara Says:

Listening and providing feedback without judgment
are indicators of true friendship.

*S*he *S*aid: I want him to be my best friend as well as my husband and lover, but he just doesn't get that.

I *S*aid: Recently, I was reminded of what a friend really is.

I was talking to my old college roommate from New York and getting her perspective on several of my own life changes. We have enjoyed a lengthy, but now long distance, friendship, and I can honestly say we know each other very well.

When we were saying our good-byes, I thanked her. She responded quickly that I did not have to thank her for anything. I explained it was a gift to me to have her simply accept me as a friend without any expectations placed on our friendship.

I further thanked her for hearing me without judgment or criticism about my choices or decisions. She explained she was honored to share her observations, opinions, and thoughts when I needed a sounding board.

This is what friends are really for, to listen and provide feedback without judgment.

When you think about your marriage or relationship, does it include friendship? If your relationship excludes day-to-day camaraderie, it is not complete. You are missing a lot.

A best friend is one you can count on in good and bad, one you can trust to accept you exactly as you came to them. A good friend does not judge or condemn your behavior and is comfortable to be around, even when you disagree.

Friendship flows between two people. One is not always giving and the other taking; the relationship between friends is weighed only by balance.

We can enjoy many acquaintances, colleagues, and neighbors who fill our world, but a true friend is rare and truly golden. And when that friend is also your lover and lifetime mate, the treasure is even greater.

He Said: Shouldn't a person feel supported by his or her mate? I don't feel like we're on the same team. In fact, I don't know if we're even in the same game.

I Said: Have you ever thought of your marriage as a team, a team of two? Any team, no matter how big or small, is only as good as its players. This applies to a marriage or relationship, doesn't it?

If both players are invested in the winning outcome of the relationship and are willing to put the effort, time, and strategy into the game, collecting the big prize is possible. If you play sports, think of the energy and alliance you bring to your team. Do you bring this same energy into winning with your partner?

Simply being together, setting similar goals, and making daily commitments to reach those goals will forge you and your partner into a team. If you include friendship into your game plan, you will create a strong and unbeatable couple.

Having a healthy relationship requires interacting on a variety of levels—as lovers, partners, friends, and yes, even teammates. To keep all interactions strong and vibrant, try having a weekly conversation to assess where you are going, individually and together. Invest the energy into your

"number one pick" that you do into other parts of your
life. To keep your joint vision alive, encourage each other
in all actions and interactions.

Enjoying each other as teammates and best friends
will initiate underlying harmony in all aspects of your
relationship.

She Said: I just want to know he understands what my days are like and the stress I'm under. Sometimes I just need him to be my best friend.

I Said: We are often quick to offer compassion and caring words to friends when they need our support and help, yet we often don't recognize that our spouse or partner could use those same considerations on a daily basis to make their life happier or brighter.

Sometimes the role of best friend is the most important role we play in our primary relationship. Little things like a quick neck rub or hug at the right time can do wonders to make our partners feel treasured. As the song goes, "Try a little tenderness."

Take time each day to be a "best friend" to your partner. Has your wife had a hard day with the kids? Wouldn't she love a few minutes alone in a frothy bath? Maybe Dad could order pizza so dinner preparation could disappear on that particularly tough day? Even better, try whisking your lady away for a few hours alone.

Guys need their wives to be their best friends, too. Jockeying for position at the office can be grueling. Threatening knocks under the hood when money is tight can be very worrisome. Even worse, the new receptionist, who is almost his age, told your man he reminded her of her father. When days filled with problems and insecurities pile up, it's time for a tender touch, cuddle, and a soothing moment with your man.

The most important thing you can be for each other is a soft place to land when life knocks you down.

He Said: Sometimes I get in trouble for laughing, but I think a good sense of humor is one of the greatest things I bring into our relationship.

I Said: In today's health conscious world, we are doing all kinds of things to prevent and decrease stress. Unfortunately, our remedies often cause even more stress.

In a marriage or relationship, there will always be stressors—children, finances, work schedules, chores, in-laws, not to mention anxiety aroused by watching the evening news. Things can get very complicated as our plates pile high.

People try various coping skills to relive stress—body massages, spa visits, fitness clubs, weekend getaways, shopping, and other recreational activities—some of which can carry a hefty price tag. It's easy to get caught in a paradox where fighting the negative consequences of stress costs money and requires a significant amount of time, which in turn leads to more stress.

There is good news! Try laughing. It's simple, cheap, easy, and makes your face look good. Yes, indeed, laughing is good for the body and soul.

A famous writer and editor for the *Saturday Review*,

Norman Cousins, was diagnosed with ankylosing spondylitis, a connective tissue disease with a poor prognosis and days filled with excruciating pain. Cousins did not want to give in to his disease, so he put himself on a personal protocol for recovery: large doses of vitamin C and loads of laughter. He did whatever he could do to make himself laugh. Jokes, mimes, humorous books, and silly television shows filled his days.

The effect was astonishing! Cousins found ten minutes of belly laughing brought a calming sensation to his pain-weary body and allowed him to live free of pain for two hours. Astonishingly enough, medical tests proved his body suffered less inflammation. Cousins' informal thesis became the first chapter in the book, *Anatomy of an Illness,* and won mention in the *New England Journal of Medicine.*

Surrounding ourselves with friends and a partner who make us laugh is good medicine for whatever ails us and offers an ounce of prevention too.

She Said: We know my illness is fatal, and, more than anything, I want him to realize that he has to take care of himself, as well. We didn't count on dealing with something like this, and it's certainly taking its toll, but I don't want our relationship to be about me dying. I want it to be about all that we've lived and experienced together.

I Said: "In sickness and in health," is an important vow we take as we marry.

We all know there may come a time when we are called upon to care for our partner if sickness or accident intrudes into our lives. Sometimes an illness progresses slowly over time and being caregiver is a role we gradually assume; sometimes health issues or disabilities show up without notice. It doesn't matter how an illness or disability disrupts our lives; the result will be the same. Care and compassion are needed.

As a partner, you may wear several hats during the healing or dying process, and some hats will fit better than others. Many times you will become the one to give much and get back little in return. At those times, it is important to surround yourself with a supportive network of family members, friends, and professionals, and take the time necessary to tend to your body and spirit, as well.

There are countless resources available to share a caregiver's responsibilities. However, many times when a loved one is suffering, the partner feels he or she is the best and only one qualified to minister to their immediate needs. Don't become a martyr as the care process extends; your effectiveness will eventually be compromised. It is important to create balance in your own life, even as you tend to the needs of your loved one.

Don't feel guilty if you take time to feel compassion for yourself. Even your "patient" will be happier if you do. Remember, your spouse or partner loves you as much as you love him or her and wants you to be whole. When someone is seriously ill, many times the only gift that person can give is permission for loved ones to go on living and enjoy their days. Accept that gift with graciousness.

Even when we are suffering, nothing is more powerful than a positive outlook followed by giving and receiving compassion, caring, and friendship.

He Said: I don't always like myself. How can I expect someone else to love me all the time?

I Said: Ask yourself an important question: Am I someone I'd like to share a relationship with?

We often get so caught up focusing on our partner that we don't look at ourselves. Isn't our first relationship supposed to be with yours truly?

We must be able to love and accept ourselves unconditionally before we can actually love another. We must be able to see our reflection with loving eyes. We must like who we are, and we must feel we are deserving of another's love. We must be able to embrace our positive and negative qualities, and like and accept the good, the bad, and the ugly.

It is with this acceptance that we are able to see love in others, which allows us to fully experience another's world.

How do you feel about yourself? Are you in love with your person? Really think about it and take a close look at the messages you send to yourself each day. Are they positive, helpful, and goal oriented? Or are they negative and self-defeating?

Are you your own best friend? Do you know what's best

for you, but sometimes do the opposite? To be in a loving relationship with another, it is important to be in one with yourself first.

Love

Barbara Says:

Love is all around us if we open our hearts to let it in.

He *Said*: She says I don't let her know I love her often enough. I'm not sure I even know what she means.

I *Said*: Telling someone you love him or her is based on your personal awareness and comfort. Some of us are better at words, some better at gestures or gifts. Whatever our ways or means, telling our loved ones we care about them will make them feel treasured.

We sometimes forget to show our loving feelings to those we hold in our heart unless the day is marked with hearts, flowers, and boxes of candy. Showing the special people in our lives they are loved, cared for, and thought about are important components needed to fashion a relationship that lasts a lifetime. Showing you care is not a one-day-a-year deal.

Instead, all year long, pay attention to what brings joy to your partner. Give according to their love language and see what magic can be conjured up. Consider that designated February heart holiday as a marker for the rest of the world and make your partner feel like a special valentine *every* day.

Whatever you do, make giving memorable and let the message "I am thinking of you" be heard loud and clear. You'll experience warm feelings, too—it makes us all feel good to make another person feel wonderful, loved, and cherished.

She Said: Sure, I love him as a person, but I'm just not in love with him anymore.

I Said: I often hear this comment from female clients. When asked to explain, this is often what I hear: "I love him because he is such a good father, has good family values, provides for us well, and spends quality time with our children. But I am not 'in love' with him."

So I ask, "Were you in love with him once?"

The answer usually follows, "Oh, of course, when we were dating and planning our wedding, it was great. We were inseparable, always had time for each other, shared common interests, and I couldn't wait to see him."

"We really enjoyed each other, and disagreements seemed rare. Now it is different. We don't have time for each other, we can't seem to complement or compliment each other, and we surely have lost 'that loving feeling.' Is it possible to get it back? I am not sure."

So what happened here? During the following counseling session, we discussed the evolution of the relationship and pinpointed the life changes that occurred. We looked at how the couple allowed external happenings and events pull them apart and how they forgot what it was like to be in love.

Love changes as people change. Events and life circumstances happen and can make it difficult to keep the love flame burning. But it can be done.

If you make an effort to remember what got you together in the first place, if you take time to reminisce about your beginnings, if you make time to "date" and be alone to reconnect, then the "being in love" feeling can return. It may not look the same, but it can feel the same and that's what makes it worthwhile.

He Said: If we loved each other like we love our chihuahua, everything would be great.

I Said: This couple said loving their chihuahua was easy because there was no conflict or arguing, and the dog showered only unconditional love on them. During counseling, they cited lack of communication as one of their problems, and both agreed they wanted to be more loving to each other.

Maybe there is a lesson to be learned from how they loved their chihuahua. Pets play a big role in our lives and provide wonderful companionship and warmth. They are easy to love, because their required emotional maintenance is so low.

What about your relationship with your mate? Do you offer unconditional love, or is the love you show based on how your partner responds to your bidding?

Is your emotional maintenance low, or are you needy and demanding, often expecting your partner to be the one to "make you happy?" Do you feel your partner should give you the life you want instead of building a life and relationship that works for both of you?

Take a tip from Rover and FiFi. If you offer companionship and warmth with realistic expectations, you may experience being truly loved and adored in return.

While people with all their complexities and needs may never be as simple and easy to love as the family pet might be, we can learn much from our four-legged friends when it comes to giving and showing love. Although loving a partner takes a lot more effort than loving a chihuahua, being loved in return by the special person in our life is well worth the effort.

She Said: I know I loved him once, but I think it's too late. I don't think we can recover from everything we've gone through.

I Said: Reclaiming love . . . yes, it can happen.

Sometimes life gets in our way, and we find we've lost, or are in danger of losing, that loving feeling we once enjoyed with our partner. Reviving romance, restoring love, and reclaiming relationships are recurring themes in any therapist's office.

Affairs, years of detachment or indifference, raising families, and/or promoting careers can cause damage, and oftentimes serious damage, to relationships. But, with a sincere commitment and effort to repair the relationship, it is possible to reconnect and restore loving feelings. The relationship can evolve into an even stronger partnership. When this happens, a higher form of love transpires.

It might be surprising, but this higher love includes a love for the world outside one's immediate partnership. By opening our hearts to humanity and placing value on love as a global emotion, we will ultimately create an emotional environment for ourselves, which will extend to our intimate relationships.

We can choose to be a loving person, instead of one who harbors hatred. We can learn how to give love unconditionally without expectations. We can do loving things to make our love active. And we can learn from our children and watch how they love and show affection.

We can search memories from the day we said "I Do" and remember why we married the wonderful person we did. Try to recall how you felt on your wedding day or on the day you knew you found the person who would make your life complete.

We can begin the very next day of our lives to reclaim our intimate relationship and take steps on the journey to a love that will last a lifetime.

He Said: She's always complaining that I don't show her I love her. I keep telling her I wouldn't still be here if I didn't. Why isn't that enough?

I Said: Don't ever assume that your partner knows you love them "just because you're there." We all experience, see, and hear love in different ways, and saying "I love you" and showing that sentiment in a variety of ways is a powerful expression reaffirming your relationship while offering a piece of who you are as well. Saying those three little words will always be exclaimed in your own individual style, but you might add these delightful innovative ways to show how much you care:

- Leave small notes in unexpected places. Wouldn't it be fun to get a note in the refrigerator saying, "Let me warm you up tonight!"

- Maybe jottings on a mirror or computer screen would bring a smile.

- Even the weekly grocery list is a fun place to write a love note. *Any place* is a good place to be playful.

- Once a month, create a day or time for just the two of you. Leading up to the special day, speak loving or teasing thoughts to build anticipation.

- Make a list of all the things you love about the special person in your life and post it where that person can see it.

- Write a love poem.

- Plan a mystery date.

- Write a love letter and send it in the mail—not in an email!

- Plan a treasure hunt leaving clues from one room to the next. The treasure can be an invitation to dinner, flowers, candy, or a love coupon.

- Cook a favorite dinner and be a loving host or hostess.

Now it's your turn. What fun or romantic ideas can you create? Let your imagination and creativity roll, so that your mate will never doubt for one moment that you absolutely love and adore him or her.

She Said: I can't remember the last time we said, "I love you" to each other. If we can't be bothered to say the words, are the feelings even there anymore?

I Said: One day, I was having a conversation with a friend, and we were talking about love. I asked my friend, "How does one know who loves more?"

My friend responded that the question really couldn't be answered, because love can't be measured. I started thinking about that idea.

We certainly can't measure love in any of the usual ways we measure things—by quarts, teaspoons, yards, inches, liters, etc.

So I thought about measuring it another way. What if we measured love by counting loving behaviors or actions? It would follow that the person performing the most loving actions would be the one that loves more.

But that didn't seem right either. If a person wasn't action oriented, where would that leave them? That brought up another question. What if a person loves quietly and introspectively? How do we quantify thoughts?

What about counting words? We could count how many times one said "I love you," but we would fall into the same trap. What if one does not believe in saying "I love you" every day, but only on special occasions?

Can it be we really can't quantify love? We can simply receive and enjoy it in all its many forms.

He Said: I don't feel about her the way I used to feel. Does that mean I don't love her as much?

I Said: Do the feelings of love stay the same or do they change as people and relationships change?

Remember what it was like when you first fell in love? Remember the emotions and feelings you had as you planned your wedding and said, "I do?" Remember how you felt as you created a home and family together?

In the early years, your feelings for each other seemed so strong that sometimes it felt as though your heart would burst with love.

Those heightened emotions are generally tempered as the years go by, and love appears to be different as people grow and change. Is it still love? Do the changes in your behavior toward each other as a couple over the years mean your love is less than it was in the beginning? Of course it doesn't.

For many couples, even after many years together, their love is still strong and deep, but it has a different as people grow together, they learn more about themselves and their life experiences expand. They become much more interesting, bringing new and different ideas into their relationship, and the definition of their love takes on new dimensions.

To understand the depth and difference of your love in the current phase of your life together, you might keep a journal and collect your feelings of love toward your spouse or partner over a period of weeks. Be certain to include personality traits, physical attributes, and acts of kindness that you see. Then refer back to your words to see how your love has grown and the many forms it takes.

The feelings you have for each other are now different than they were in your beginning together. Don't feel love is no longer there; it has simply morphed into a different package. If you're not sure you love your mate, think about your life without them. What would it be like? If you know something special would be missing from your life if your partner was no longer there, your love has simply taken on a different form.

She Said: He assures me he loves me, but most of the time he doesn't tell me or even act like he loves me.

I Said: Affection is one of the most important elements of a relationship. For many, it's the best part of being with someone. How affectionate are you in your relationship? Do you show your love, as well as verbally express your love?

I love silly words of affection like, "Hey lady of mine, you really look hot today!" Words like "I love you and care about you," really make my head spin. But little things like holding hands or intimately touching a shoulder, a gentle touch to a cheek, or opening the car door speak just as loudly as words and reaffirm that the spoken words of love are actually true.

Even though you may often think warm snuggly thoughts about the one you love, if those thoughts are not turned into words or actions, your partner doesn't have the pleasure of experiencing them. Thinking affectionately is wonderful, but how will your loved one know what you are thinking if you don't tell or show him or her?

At the end of each day, think about how you expressed affection for the one you love and care about. Then make your plan for tomorrow!

He *Said*: She just doesn't get it. I am not sure I love her enough to stay.

I *Said*: What if life doesn't bring you exactly what you want and you can't get it, no matter how hard you try? What do you do? Give up? Settle for what you have? Decide it really isn't worth going for the gold? Or do you expect someone else to make things happen for you?

Nonsense. None of those choices is in your best interest. You can create your own moments, write your own scenes, and make it happen, both for yourself and for your relationship. You owe yourself all attempts to make your life choices work.

When I see a couple teetering on the brink of divorce, I usually ask what brings them to counseling and I get varied responses. Sometimes one in the couple wants to save the marriage, sometimes one comes because the other mandated it.

I counsel couples they can always get a divorce, that's easy, but why not try to save their marriage first? By putting time and energy into creating moments of connection and truly looking at what they have together, the couple will then be able to decide if what they can create together will meet their needs, both individually and as a couple.

Try everything to create moments of fulfillment and connection, both personally and as a couple. Do not give up on yourself or your relationship because "it's not working." What isn't working? Define it, talk about it, look at possible solutions to problems, and then create moments and responses that work best for you.

Don't have tunnel vision when it comes to your life or your relationship. Be willing to look around, see what different choices you can make individually and together, and then go for it. Use your time to create moments that help your life and relationship bloom and prosper.

Be your own best friend and give yourself the very advice you would give a special friend.

Listen to your words of advice and put them into action. Our minutes on this planet are special and every one counts. So let this be the first of your special moments.

One Final "I Said"

Nothing worth anything ever comes easy.

It is now up to you to assess how important your relationship is to you. And if it comes out as number one, go for it with all you have.

I wish you love, life, and happiness in all your future endeavors with the special someone in your life.

About the Author

Author Barbara Peters has a bachelor of arts degree in sociology from C.W. Post College of Long Island University, a bachelor of science in nursing from Stony Brook University, and a masters of science in counseling from Georgia State. As a nurse and counselor, Barbara has worked in diverse settings managing behavioral health organizations, psychiatric hospitals, and employee assistance consulting firms. She is certified by the National Board of Certified Counselors and a member of Licensed Professional Counselors of Georgia.

Her passion is working with couples, utilizing a solution-focused approach channeled with optimism as she guides

PHOTO BY PHIL WINTER PHOTOGRAPHY

couples toward developing a stronger relationship. She also works with individuals in a variety of other areas.

"My counseling style is interactive, respectful, non-judgmental, and supportive. With gentle questioning, I help people get in touch with their own values and ideals to gain trust in themselves to make decisions for a better lifestyle," Barbara states.

Originally from Long Island, Barbara has made Georgia her home for the last twenty-four years. Her private counseling practice is located in Cumming, and she lives in Big Canoe. Barbara is devoted to her family that includes her husband, two grown daughters, four grandchildren, and a Shih Tzu named GingerLily that often accompanies her to work.

Please visit her website at www.bjpcounseling.com.